UNIT 3

SRA Open Court Reading

Science Cycles

Grade 1

McGraw Hill Education

Program Authors

Carl Bereiter, Ph.D.
Andrew Biemiller, Ph.D.
Joe Campione, Ph.D.
Doug Fuchs, Ph.D.
Lynn Fuchs, Ph.D.
Steve Graham, Ph.D.
Karen Harris, Ph.D.
Jan Hirshberg, Ed.D.
Anne McKeough, Ph.D.
Marsha Roit, Ed.D.
Marlene Scardamalia, Ph.D.
Marcy Stein, Ph.D.
Gerald H. Treadway Jr, Ph.D.

Photo Credits

26 blphoto/Alamy; **27** Bruce Fritz/USDA-ARS; **28** ©Pixtal/age fotostock; **28-29** Marek Mnich/Getty Images; **29** Gary John Norman/Lifesize/Getty Images; **30** 3sbworld/Getty Images; **30-31** Imagemore/Glow Images; **31** Sandy Tidy Photography/Getty Images; **32** Designpics.com/PunchStock; **32-33** Ingram Publishing; **33** Digital Vision/Getty Images; **34** Thinkstock Images/Jupiterimages/Comstock Images; **34-35** Wetzel and Company; **35** Kazuhiko Kikuchi/Aflo/Getty Images; **36** Medioimages/PunchStock; **37** Jacques Cornell / McGraw-Hill Education, Bear Dancer Studios/Mark Dierker, Digital Vision/Getty Images; **38** Artyom Rudenko/Getty Images; **38-39** michaklootwijk/Getty Images; **39** PBNJ Productions/Getty Images; **40** IMAGEMORE Co.,Ltd./Getty Images; **41** Martin Ruegner/Photodisc/Getty Images; **42** U.S. Fish & Wildlife Service; **43** Wind Home Photography/Getty Images; **44** Hans Lang/Getty Images; **45** ©IT Stock Free/Alamy; **46** Vitalii Hulai/Getty Images; **47** Ablestock/Jupiterimages; **51** Cultura Creative/Alamy, RyanKing999/Getty Images, Nikolaj Schouboe/Getty Images. **Back Cover:** tBoyan/E+/Getty Images, tBoyan/E+/Getty Images, tBoyan/E+/Getty Images.

MHEonline.com

McGraw Hill Education

Send all inquiries to:
McGraw-Hill Education
8787 Orion Place
Columbus, OH 43240

ISBN: 978-0-07-668799-2
MHID: 0-07-668799-6

Printed in the United States of America.

8 9 GPC 24

UNIT 3

Science Cycles

Book 2

Table of Contents

Essential Question What happens to water after it rains?

Journey of a Raindrop

by Vidas Barzdukas
illustrated by Cale Atkinson

The tiny raindrops lived in the clouds. The clouds grew dark. "It is going to rain!" a raindrop said.

The raindrops grew bigger. They became heavier. The clouds could not hold them anymore. So the raindrops fell to Earth. "Here we go!" the raindrops cheered.

Quickly the raindrops fell. Splash!
A raindrop fell on a flower. Plop!
A raindrop fell in the dirt. Pitter patter!
The raindrops tumbled all around.

The dirt sipped the silver raindrops. The flowers drank in the cool water. A bubbling brook called to the raindrops. "Let's go on a trip!"

The raindrops joined the brook. Together they rushed over glittering pebbles and around shiny stones. They lapped at the grass growing on the shore.

"Over there!" a raindrop said. Ahead, the brook joined a large stream. The stream curled around tiny islands of rock and grass.

More brooks joined the swollen stream. More raindrops fell from the stormy sky. Some of the raindrops joined the stream to go on the trip.

Children splashed in the cool water. Two sailboats sailed along the shore. A golden fish darted around a rock as an eagle soared high overhead.

The stream poured into the ocean. The ocean was wide and deep. Giant ships cut through the waves. The raindrops smiled as the giant ships blew their horns.

"Is this the end of the trip?" a raindrop asked. "Does our trip end here in the ocean?"

Suddenly, the dark clouds parted. The sun shone down big and bright over the blue water.

"Your trip does not end here," the sun said to the raindrops. "There is another part of the trip you must take. Are you ready?"

The air grew warmer and warmer. Slowly, the tiny raindrops became a mist. The mist rose up into the sky.

A cool wind changed the mist back into raindrops. The raindrops then joined hands to make clouds.

"You are part of the water cycle," the sun said to the raindrops. "A cycle happens over and over again."

"Water changes," the sun said. "Water can be oceans, brooks, and rivers. It can be lakes and streams."

"When water warms up, it turns into a gas like mist or steam," the sun said. "Think of a puddle. After a rainstorm, my heat warms the puddles. They get smaller and smaller as they evaporate."

"When the gas, or evaporated water, cools, it becomes drops of water. The drops of water form clouds."

The sun told the tired raindrops to close their eyes and nap. They were happy to sleep in the cloud until it was time for the cycle to start again.

The water cycle is nature's way to circulate water around the Earth.

Essential Question Why is springtime rain important for nature?

Spring Rain

by Elena Vasquez
illustrated by Audrey Durney

Spring rain warms the cold ground.
See the raindrops as they fall down.
The water slowly slips into the soil.
It nudges the plant and flower seeds;
Reminds them to spread out their roots.

It is time to send out
the song of spring time:
Grow, grow, grow!

Essential Question What changes do you see when watching a flower grow?

From Seed to Flower

by Jeri Cipriano

Look at all the beautiful sunflowers. Do you know how sunflowers grow? They start as seeds.

You can grow your own sunflowers from seeds. Let's see how.

The first thing you need to do is buy sunflower seeds. Where do you get seeds? You can buy a package of seeds at the garden store.

Now find a place to plant the seeds. You will need a place with plenty of space and soft soil. You will also need a small shovel.

Next, dig holes in the soil in a row. Drop the seeds into the holes and cover them up with soil. Now you must water the seeds.

It will take time for the seeds to grow into sunflowers. Make sure you water the seeds every day. Pull out any weeds that grow near the seeds.

Soon, roots will grow out of the seeds into the ground. They soak up the water you give them. The water helps the sunflowers grow stems and leaves.

Finally tiny stems sprout up through the soil. The stems have tiny leaves on them. Make sure to keep giving the stems plenty of water!

Every day the stems grow taller and taller. Look! What is next to that leaf? That is a bud. Buds are the flowers that are not open yet. The bud will bloom into a big, beautiful flower.

Look! The bud is starting to open, and a flower is starting to grow. Soon all the buds will open. Then there will be many sunflowers.

The sunflowers are in full bloom.
Each flower has pretty, yellow petals.

Just imagine! These large, beautiful flowers came from tiny seeds. The cycle of seeds becoming plants repeats over and over. Isn't that amazing?

Essential Question How do animals change as they grow older?

Insects Grow and Change

by Katie Sharp

Insects are animals. All animals grow and change. Some insects do not change very much from when they are born. This grasshopper does not change a lot.

Other insects change a great deal as they grow. They look different at each stage in their lives. Sometimes they change inside a protective case called a chrysalis that they form around themselves.

Does a bee always look like a bee? No, a new bee, called a larva, looks more like a worm. Adult bees take care of the larva. They build a waxy covering over it.

As the larva ages it becomes a pupa. It continues to grow inside a sack called a cocoon. Over time, the baby bee grows more body parts until the new adult bee chews out of the wax.

Is a butterfly always a butterfly? No, it is a caterpillar when it hatches from an egg. A caterpillar does not have wings and cannot fly. It crawls among plants and eats their leaves.

The hungry caterpillar grows as it eats. Then it makes a hard covering to protect itself as it changes into a butterfly. When the butterfly comes out, it has colorful wings!

Does a beetle always look like a beetle? No, most new beetles, called larvae, look like worms first. Larvae come out of eggs.

A larva grows and grows. It sheds its skin many times. In time it grows a hard covering to protect its adult beetle body.

When a dragonfly egg hatches, the larva is called a nymph. It lives in or near the water and grows until it is ready to shed its skin and become a dragonfly.

This is an adult dragonfly. Look at his wings! They grew while he was a nymph. Insects grow and change in many amazing ways!

Essential Question How do living things change as they grow?

Cycles of Life

by Oliver Rodriguez
illustrated by Dave Kirwan

A seed and a tadpole
start off small.
But it won't be long
until they grow tall.

Wiggle, wiggle,
swim, and jump!
The tadpole grows from an egg
to a frog sitting on a stump.

Grow, grow, grow
roots and stem!
Leaves spread from the branches,
perhaps fruit will grow from them.

The life cycle of a frog.
The life cycle of a tree.
What a fun journey for us to see!

Glossary

A

along
in a direction toward something else

C

change
to become different

cycle
a set of events or actions that happen again and again in the same order; a repeating series

E

evaporate
to go from a liquid to a gas

P

plant
to put a seed, flower, or plant in the ground to grow

plenty
a large amount

S

shed
to lose or get rid of leaves, skin, or fur naturally

soil
the top layer of earth in which plants grow

sprout
to grow

stage
a specific point in the development of something

T

themselves
their own selves